]

The True Story of Edward Snowden

By Cliff Kincaid

Cliff Kincaid, a veteran journalist and media critic, is the founder and president of America's Survival, Inc. (ASI), a public policy organization with an established track record of fighting global Jihad, the International Communist Movement, and the United Nations. ASI is currently working to reestablish Congressional committees or subcommittees to investigate internal security problems.

Martin Edwin Andersen, a former senior adviser for policy planning at the Criminal Division of the U.S. Department of Justice, was the first national security whistleblower to be given the U.S. Office of Special Counsel's "Public Servant Award." Andersen had suffered a series of retaliatory measures for blowing the whistle about leaks of highly classified information, sexual harassment, sexual favoritism in hiring, violations of travel rules, general mismanagement, and other wrongdoing at the Justice Department under Attorney General Janet Reno.

America's Survival, Inc.
P. O. Box 146, Owings, MD 20736

www.usasurvival.org   443-964-8208

Table of Contents

Senator Rand Paul's Snowden Problem

This book examines the strange case of NSA defector Edward Snowden, his associates and collaborators. While his disclosures have clearly aided and abetted America's enemies, he has been hailed as a hero by some prominent conservatives and libertarians such as Kentucky Republican Senator Rand Paul, a likely 2016 presidential candidate.

As the 2016 presidential campaign gets underway, the enormous damage done by Snowden's disclosures may well undermine Senator Paul's anticipated run for the White House. Paul was not only a supporter of the leaker but adopted his anti-NSA campaign in Congress.

Paul compared Snowden to Henry David Thoreau and Martin Luther King, Jr. during an appearance on Fox News' Sean Hannity show. Paul said about Snowden, "On deciding when you decide to become a civil disobedient—we've had famous ones in our career, but some of them only had to serve, like [Henry David] Thoreau only had to serve one day in jail, Martin Luther King served 30 days in jail."

Former officials of the NSA have generally refused to comment on politicians by name. But some are speaking out regarding how Snowden's disclosures have made it easier for our enemies and adversaries to wage war against us.

Former NSA executive Charlie Speight published a

blog post under the headline, "Rand Paul: Putin's Best Friend." Speight lambasted Paul's anti-NSA rhetoric and actions, saying, "Buying into the uneducated, no-deeper-than-headlines 'scandal' claiming NSA collecting everyone's cell phone calls, texts and emails, Paul has decided to attack one of America's greatest assets."

He said the result of the anti-NSA campaign "has been to damage the reputation of the single most successful and important intelligence organization in the world. That means, the organization most feared by our adversaries, primarily Russia, China, North Korea, Iran and terrorists."

He argued that Paul "is directly enhancing the fortunes of our adversaries, weakening the U.S.'s best interests and putting our country—and her troops—at risk. Rand Paul is becoming an accomplice of Edward Snowden and becoming Vladimir Putin's and Xi Jinping's, Kim Jung-Un's, Hassan Rouhani's and Al Qaeda's best friend."

Some may consider these comments a natural defense of an agency that once employed Speight. But it appears that our enemies and adversaries also acknowledge the damage Snowden has done.

Zhang Zhaozhong, professor at the People's Liberation Army (PLA) National Defense University, is quoted in the pro-China *Global Times* as saying, "The damage to the U.S. of Edward Snowden's flight equals the loss of 10 heavy armored divisions."

Snowden's "flight," of course, was to Russia through Hong Kong, China.

In his book, *No Place to Hide: Edward Snowden, the NSA and the U.S. Surveillance State,* Greenwald admits that Snowden picked Hong Kong because it was "part of Chinese territory" and that "American agents would find it harder to operate against him there…"

Researcher Nevin Gussack says the Zhaozhong quote is "more of a statement on the impact of an NSA contract employee who posed as a whistleblower and human/civil rights campaigner," one "who portrayed himself as a victim of the big, bad, evil national security state." Snowden's campaign, Gussack argues, has diverted attention from "the very real threat of Sino-Russian cyber-warfare and other aggressive activities directed at the U.S. It also gives the U.S. a black eye internationally, as well as galvanizing the leftists and the 'antiwar' elements amongst the 'conservatives' and left-libertarians to cripple the functions of the national security organs." He says the professor's use of the "ten divisions" term is meant to characterize "a knockout blow to an enemy," a "well-placed, well-timed psychological attack" on the United States that would "cripple our resistance and contribute to our defeat as a power without firing a volley of bullets."

The comments preceded what the FBI described as a North Korean cyber attack on Sony pictures which destroyed systems and stole large quantities of personal and commercial data.

Admiral Michael S. Rogers, Commander of the U.S. Cyber Command and Director of the National Security Agency, spoke about cyber warfare during testimony before the House Intelligence Committee. The Reuters news agency account said Rogers' testimony included a warning that China and "probably one or two" other countries have the ability through cyber warfare to disrupt or possibly shut down computer systems of U.S. power utilities, aviation networks and financial companies.

So while our media—and politicians like Rand Paul—have been waging war on the NSA, our enemies have been figuring out how to exploit Snowden's disclosures.

Consider the invasion of Ukraine. "Some U.S. military and intelligence officials say Russia's war planners might have used knowledge about the U.S.'s usual surveillance techniques to change communication methods about the looming invasion" of Ukraine, the *Wall Street Journal* said on March 24, 2013. The story never mentioned Edward Snowden. Clearly, however, the "knowledge" about U.S. surveillance techniques came from Snowden.

The paper said, "America's vaunted global surveillance is a vital tool for U.S. intelligence services, especially as an early-warning system and as a way to corroborate other evidence. In Crimea, though, U.S. intelligence officials are concluding that Russian planners might have gotten a jump on the West by evading U.S. eavesdropping."

In Crimea's capital, Putin's supporters were seen rallying around a statue of Lenin. Some were carrying pictures of Stalin. Snowden is their hero, too.

As if there were any doubt about Snowden's services and his new boss, he fled to Russia and then appeared on a national Russian TV show, giving Vladimir Putin a softball question: "Does Russia intercept, store or analyze in any way the communications of millions of individuals? And do you believe that simply increasing the effectiveness of intelligence or law enforcement investigations can justify placing societies, rather than their subjects, under surveillance?" To no one's surprise, Putin denied it, saying, "On such a mass scale ... we do not allow ourselves to do this, and we will never allow this. We do not have the money or the means to do that," he said.

Stephen Stromberg, a *Post* editorial writer, noted that Snowden had "played a set piece in Vladimir Putin's latest act of propaganda..." But the damage goes much deeper than that. The Post itself was an outlet for Snowden's anti-NSA disclosures.

Espionage and Not Journalism

Steve Coll, dean of the Graduate School of Journalism at Columbia University, wrote a story that carried the title of "How Edward Snowden Changed Journalism. [1]" But the article didn't live up to its billing. The author didn't want his readers to understand that journalism has changed into a form of espionage that benefits the Islamic terrorists anxious to kill us. To use President Obama's phrase, you might call it the "fundamental transformation" of journalism. Coll could not bring himself to report the truth because Columbia had bestowed prestigious journalism awards—the Pulitzers—on the recipients of Snowden's stolen national security documents.

At a news conference, my group, America's Survival, Inc., had called the Snowden awards "Pulitzer Prizes for Espionage. [2]" We noted that Joseph Pulitzer left $2 million to establish the Columbia Journalism School, saying he wanted journalism to have a positive moral influence on society. He said, "I am deeply interested in the progress and elevation of journalism, having spent my life in that profession, regarding it as a noble profession and one of unequaled importance for its influence upon the minds and morals of the people. I desire to assist in attracting to this profession young men of character and ability, also to help those already engaged in the profession to acquire the highest moral and intellectual training."

How moral is it to receive stolen documents from someone who is at least an agent of Russia and may, in fact, have been a spy all along?

Ignoring Snowden's life in Moscow, in the loving embrace of Vladimir Putin, Steve Coll also failed to report that one of the Pulitzer Prize recipients, Glenn Greenwald, has an affinity for governments, groups and movements opposing the United States. Greenwald spoke publicly in favor of "weakening" America, saying that al-Qaeda's 9/11 terrorist attacks were "very minimal in scope compared to the level of deaths that the United States has been bringing to the world for decades—from Vietnam to illegal wars in Central America…" [3] Greenwald described Anwar al-Awlaki, the American al-Qaeda leader killed in a drone strike, merely as "someone who the U.S. government hates because he speaks effectively to the Muslim world about the violence that the United States commits regionally, and the responsibility of Muslims to stand up to that violence." Al-Awlaki inspired the Fort Hood massacre, in which 13 were killed.

Greenwald's record also includes collaborating with Leninist groups such as the International Socialist Organization, and Islamist organizations such as the Council on American-Islamic Relations (CAIR), a Muslim Brotherhood front. The Muslim Brotherhood is a global Sunni Muslim movement that seeks to spread Sharia` or Islamic law around the world.

Coll seemed to go out of his way to obscure what Snowden and his collaborators were doing. He highlighted that Snowden took steps "to protect his data and his communications with journalists made it possible for the Guardian and the [Washington] Post to publish their initial stories and bring Snowden to global attention."

Coll pretends not to understand that these are the hallmarks of an espionage operation. It was not an accident that even the Obama administration has indicted Snowden for espionage. Obama may not have favored such an indictment, but the national security establishment certainly did.

Coll wrote about Snowden's disclosures, saying, "In fashioning balanced practices for reporters, it is critical to ask how often and in what ways governments—ours and others—systematically target journalists' communications in intelligence collection. For all his varied revelations about surveillance, this is an area where Snowden's files have been less than definitive."

He is mostly referring to alleged NSA surveillance of American journalists. But who, or what, are those "other" governments? And isn't it safe to assume that Snowden is under surveillance and control by the Russian secret police?

Described as a reporter "on issues of intelligence and national security in the United States and abroad," Coll has too much experience in this area not to recognize the truth about the Snowden espionage operation.

Yes, journalism has changed, and all it takes to understand the change is to visit the Columbia Journalism building, which contains a plaque saying their mission is to "uphold standards of excellence in journalism."

"Our Republic and its press will rise or fall together," Joseph Pulitzer wrote, also on a plaque inside the Columbia Journalism building.

But today's elite journalists don't seem to care if the country falls, even though their own rights would disappear in the process.

The theft was breathtaking. A classified report from the Department of Defense (DoD) concluded that Snowden downloaded approximately 1.7 million intelligence files—described as the single largest theft of secrets in the history of the United States—and that "much of the information stolen by Snowden is related to current U.S. military operations."

Matt Olsen, who led the National Counterterrorism Center, said that Snowden's stolen and leaked documents "changed the way terrorists communicate, causing them to fall out of the U.S. government's sight." He added, "They've changed how they encrypt their communications and adopted more stringent encryption techniques," Olsen said. "They've changed service providers and email addresses and they've, in some cases, just dropped off altogether."

NSA's former deputy director, Chris Inglis, talked about the problem in a *Washington Times* article [4] about how ISIS is "using leaked Snowden info to evade U.S. intelligence." Reporter Rowan Scarborough said Snowden's "top-secret disclosures" are the key to making the Islamic State killers "harder to find because they know how to avoid detection."

A major study demonstrated how Snowden has in fact helped the Islamists. The firm Recorded Future said that, "Following the June 2013 Edward Snowden leaks we observe an increased pace of innovation, specifically new competing jihadist platforms and three major new encryption tools from three (3) different organizations—GIMF, Al-Fajr Technical Committee, and ISIS—within a three to five-month time frame of the leaks."

Speaking before the Senate Armed Services Committee on February 11, 2014, Defense Intelligence Agency (DIA) Director Lt. Gen. Michael T. Flynn said, "In my professional military judgment Mr. Snowden's disclosures have done grave damage to the Department of Defense and go far beyond the act of a so-called whistleblower. I have no doubt that he has placed the men and women of our armed services at risk and that his disclosures will cost lives on our future battlefields." Flynn said Snowden's theft of documents has made it harder for U.S. troops to avoid being maimed or killed by terrorist bombs known as improvised explosive devices (IEDs).

The implication is that Snowden's disclosures will increase the likelihood of more "wounded warriors" from conflicts in the Middle East and around the world.

He went on to say, "...I won't put a dollar figure but I know that the scale or the cost to our nation obviously in treasure, in capabilities that are going to have to be examined, reexamined, and potentially adjusted, but I think that the greatest cost that is unknown today, but we will likely face, is the cost in human lives on tomorrow's battlefield or in some, someplace where we will put our military forces—you know, when we ask them to go into harm's way. That's the greatest cost that we face with the disclosures that have been presented so far. And like I said, the strongest word that I can use is this has caused grave damage to our national security."

In terms of the harm and financial cost, former CIA officer Robert Baer said about Snowden, "...this guy has done more damage to U.S. intelligence than I've seen anybody do. And he's gone way beyond this brief of, you know, protecting privacy of Americans...It's going to cost us billions."

On another occasion, Baer said, "...ISIS has been reading Snowden...they know to stay off phones, stay off e-mail and the rest of it. They're communicating with mobile Wi-Fi. They can beat the National Security Agency..."

When the terrorists beat the NSA, that means it is more likely they will be able to kill Americans. Since Snowden's disclosures, we have seen major Islamic terror attacks around the world.

Rep. Mike Rogers, when he was chairman of the House Intelligence Committee, and Rep. C.A. Dutch Ruppersberger (MD), the ranking Democrat on the Intelligence Committee, released a statement describing Snowden's "acts of betrayal," which they said "truly place America's military men and women in greater danger around the world." They issued a joint bipartisan statement [5] saying that a Department of Defense assessment of the damage caused by Snowden's disclosures had confirmed that Snowden downloaded approximately 1.7 million intelligence files, the single largest theft of secrets in the history of the United States, and that much of the information stolen by Snowden is related to current U.S. military operations.

They said Snowden's theft and leaking of U.S. classified material has the potential to jeopardize the lives of real American military men and women working overseas, and risks the failure of current US military operations. They said Snowden's disclosures have already tipped off our adversaries to the sources and methods of our defense, and hurt U.S. allies helping us with counter terrorism, cybercrime, human and narcotics trafficking, and the proliferation of weapons of mass destruction.

Steve Coll's article purported to be a review of a film about Snowden, who comes across "as shrewd, tough, and hard to read." In fact, Snowden was a Ron Paul supporter who should never have gotten a security clearance at the CIA or NSA. Like Glenn Greenwald, who began his career with the libertarian Cato Institute, Snowden apparently had some libertarian tendencies.

But if there were any doubt about Snowden's allegiances, it should be remembered that in his statement from Moscow international airport, he said that the countries which have stood "against human rights violations carried out by the powerful rather than the powerless," and which offered him "support and asylum," included Russia, Venezuela, Bolivia, Nicaragua, and Ecuador. They had his "gratitude and respect."

Whatever the state of his current ideology, Snowden and his collaborators made it their mission to undermine U.S. national security by cooperating with America's adversaries and enemies.

The problem was getting too big to ignore. Politico's Michael Hersh observed, "...the international environment has changed dramatically for the worse since the first Snowden revelations. The horrifying rise of what may be al Qaeda's even more barbaric successor, the Islamic State, along with new threats from Russian President Vladimir Putin and others, has reoriented discussion back toward the perils that the NSA programs were intended to thwart in the first place."

The obvious flaw in this story is the failure to directly connect the dots—from Snowden's disclosures to the foreign threats and problems being discussed. Do the media want to pretend that all of this is just an accident?

America's Security Meltdown

President Obama's 30-year history of associating with unsavory characters, beginning with communist Frank Marshall Davis and continuing with Jeremiah Wright and communist terrorists Bill Ayers and Bernardine Dohrn, should have disqualified him from getting a security clearance in the government that he runs. But he didn't need to get a security clearance. Candidates for federal office, in contrast to federal employment, do not undergo any background checks at all.

Former FBI supervisor Max Noel has pointed out that the FBI once utilized a CARL test when it conducted background checks on people for high-level positions. The acronym CARL stands for Character, Associates, Reputation, and Loyalty. He says Obama could not have passed the test.

In the case of Snowden, the Office of Personnel Management used the firm U.S. Investigations Services to provide a background check. It was clearly deficient.

The questionnaire for national security positions is a 127-page document. Standard Form 86, or the "Questionnaire for National Security Positions." It asks for such information as relatives and associates, foreign activities, foreign countries visited, the use of illegal drugs, and involvement in groups dedicated to terrorism or the overthrow of the U.S. government.

The State Department says, "Eligibility for access to classified information, commonly known as a security clearance, is granted only to those for whom an appropriate personnel security background investigation has been completed. It must be determined that the individual's personal and professional history indicates loyalty to the United States, strength of character, trustworthiness, honesty, reliability, discretion, and sound judgment, as well as freedom from conflicting allegiances and potential for coercion, and a willingness and ability to abide by regulations governing the use, handling, and protection of classified information."

Yet, when questions were raised about Huma Abedin, a top aide to then-Secretary of State Hillary Clinton, no evidence emerged that she had even filled one out. Abedin had family connections to the Muslim Brotherhood, as well as to Saudi Arabia, where she once lived and was raised.

The NSA has itself been badly damaged by spy scandals over the years.

Retired FBI special agent John Whiteside tells a dramatic story of NSA espionage in his book, *Fool's Mate*, which examines the case of Robert Lipka. He betrayed his country for cash from the Soviet KGB. On September 24, 1997, more than 30 years after his crime of betrayal, Lipka was sentenced to 18 years in prison. [6]

Two previous NSA defectors to the Soviet Union/Russia, Bernon F. Mitchell and William H. Martin, were exposed as perverts. Mitchell confessed to "sexual experimentation with dogs and chickens," according to the 1962 House Committee on Un-American Activities report, *Security Practices in the National Security Agency.* Mitchell, who had "associations with members of the Communist Party," was "sexually abnormal," had "posed for nude color slides perched on a velvet-covered stool," and had "homosexual problems." The report said Mitchell and Martin "had supposedly gone through the most rigorous of loyalty and security checks prior to and during their employment with the most sensitive and secretive of all agencies"—the NSA.

At that time, the government frowned on employing homosexuals and "deviates." In fact, a 1950 congressional report was titled, *Employment of Homosexuals and Other Sex Perverts in Government,* and said that the FBI, the CIA, and the intelligence services of the Army, Navy and Air Forces were all "in complete agreement that sex perverts in government constitute security risks."

Today, the NSA has "Special Emphasis Programs" that are in place for various groups, including the "Gay, Lesbian, Bisexual, and Transgender (GLBT)." Examples of presentations NSA has sponsored include, "Can We Talk: Gay and Straight Issues in the Workplace."

Back in 2000, Reed Irvine and I wrote an article

about homosexual Rep. Barney Frank, who was reprimanded by the House over a sex scandal, being invited to speak to CIA employees. "Down the road," we said, "the CIA and the National Security Agency, which also sent open gays to hear Barney Frank, may recruit men who dress as women, and vice versa. After all, the transgendered also want their rights."

It has all come to pass, under America's first gay president, as *Newsweek* called Obama.

Open homosexual Bradley Manning, a former Army intelligence analyst, was convicted of espionage for stealing and leaking classified information to WikiLeaks. He was a public homosexual activist in the Armed Forces for at least over a year. During this time he apparently came up with the idea of downloading and releasing the classified information to WikiLeaks as a way to get back at the United States military over its policy regarding homosexuality.

President Obama had promised during the 2008 campaign to repeal the homosexual exclusion policy and in office has championed the "rights" of homosexual and "transgendered" people to high-level federal positions.

In a clear indication that the law was being ignored by the Obama Administration, the evidence demonstrates that Manning was continuing to serve after openly flaunting his homosexuality, including on Facebook. It was only later that the homosexual exclusion policy was overturned.

Who in the Obama Administration—and the Department of Defense—was aware of his conduct and looked the other way? Was Manning given a pass because his "lifestyle" was considered to be in favor and acceptable under the Obama Administration?

Lt. Col. Robert K. Brown, editor and publisher of *Soldier of Fortune Magazine*, asks the pertinent question, "How did Manning get a security clearance? Many years ago, during my first tour in the Army, I was a Special Agent in the Counter Intelligence Corps. Most of the time I ran security background checks on those that were being considered for security clearances. If the check on him was done like we did it, all this crap the NYT has dredged up would have outed this guy early on. So, the real question is, who ran the BI (background investigation) on him…?"

John Barron, in his book, *KGB: The Secret Work of Soviet Secret Agents*, said the following:

> "Contrary to popular supposition, the KGB is not primarily interested in homosexuals because of their presumed susceptibility to blackmail.

> "In its judgment, homosexuality often is accompanied by personality disorders that make the victim potentially unstable and vulnerable to adroit manipulation. It hunts the

particular homosexual who, while more or less a functioning member of his society, is nevertheless subconsciously at war with it and himself.

"Compulsively driven into tortured relations that never gratify, he cannot escape awareness that he is different. Being different, he easily rationalizes that he is not morally bound by the mores, values, and allegiances that unite others in community and society. Moreover, he nurtures a dormant impulse to strike back at the society which he feels has conspired to make him a secret leper. To such a man, treason offers the weapon of retaliation."

Manning leaked classified information to Wikileaks.org website and its founder, the strange character known as Julian Assange. Assange received asylum in the Ecuadorian embassy in London because he feared being sent by the British to Sweden to answer sex charges and then eventually extradited to the U.S. to answer espionage charges here.

Trevor Loudon's report for America's Survival, Inc., "Julian Assange: Whistleblower or Spy for Moscow?," looked at how Assange has served the interests of the Kremlin. In Russia, Assange is regarded as a hero for his charges and disclosures damaging to America and its allies. He even went to work for the Russian government, which gave him a visa and a television show on the Russia Today (RT) propaganda channel.

Before going to work for RT, Assange had told the pro-Russian government Izvestia newspaper, "We have [compromising materials] about Russia, about your government and businessmen. But not as much as we'd like... We will publish these materials soon." Another WikiLeaks spokesperson, Kristinn Hrafnsson, was quoted as saying, "Russians are going to find out a lot of interesting facts about their country." But none of that materialized. The Russian intelligence agency had warned WikiLeaks not to release anything embarrassing to Russia.

Another lie was told when Assange had insisted that he had no contact with Manning, when evidence at Manning's preliminary hearing demonstrated correspondence and communication between the two.

Yet, Manning had supporters on the left and right, including former Congressman Ron Paul, who called him a "hero." For his part, Assange said, "In relation to Rand Paul: well, I'm a big admirer of Ron Paul and Rand Paul for their very principled positions in the U.S. Congress on a number of issues." He went on, "They have been the strongest supporters with the fight against the U.S. attack on WikiLeaks and on me in the U.S. Congress."

Assange also praised Matt Drudge of the Drudge Report for being "a news media innovator" and "breaking a lot of the censorship." The America's Survival, Inc. report, "How Alex Jones Serves Vladimir Putin's War Propaganda Apparatus and

Plays a Key Role in Russian 'Active Measures' Operations," notes extensive links between Matt Drudge and Alex Jones.

Jones had appeared on the RT propaganda channel with regularity, even to defend the Russian invasion of the independent country of Georgia, a former Soviet republic. He said Russia had been provoked by the U.S. "private international military industrial complex," which had "launched a sneak attack" on the "Russian enclaves" in Georgia in order to support the "U.S.-backed Georgians [and] the Israeli- and NATO-backed Georgians."

In using Alex Jones, the Kremlin's purpose is obvious—to create the impression that the United States is being controlled by sinister forces that want to exploit the world and start wars for nefarious reasons.

The Snowdenistas

Leftist filmmaker Oliver Stone is planning a film this year glorifying Snowden. In addition, the stewards of the James Bond movie franchise, Michael Wilson and Barbara Broccoli, are producing a movie based on Glenn Greenwald's book about Edward Snowden's theft and leaking of top-secret U.S. surveillance documents, *No Place to Hide: Edward Snowden, the NSA and the U.S. Surveillance State.*

The film on Snowden that has already been released, "Citizenfour,"[7] showed the former NSA analyst in Hong Kong, China, after arranging through encrypted messages to meet his collaborators and spill his stolen NSA documents. What the film describes is an espionage operation to damage America and our allies.

For obvious reasons, Snowden's most important collaborator and current sponsor, Russian President Vladimir Putin, doesn't make an appearance in the film.

"Citizenfour" was directed by Laura Poitras, perhaps the central figure in the NSA leaks controversy, even more important than Greenwald. She says she "has been detained and interrogated about her work at the U.S. border over 40 times." Greenwald has claimed that the Department of Homeland Security has been behind her detentions and interrogations.

In a New York Times interview, she said she had

been placed on a "Watch List" by the U.S. Government since 2006, and claims she has been trying to find out why, with the assistance of the ACLU.[8]

John McCormack, a staff writer for The Weekly Standard, reported evidence that Poitras, who has been covering the wars in the Middle East, "had foreknowledge of a November 20, 2004 ambush of U.S. troops [in Iraq] but did nothing to warn them." He said a Joint Terrorism Task Force investigation was launched about the attack, but that no charges were filed against Poitras.

Nevertheless, the blog Think Progress hailed Poitras for making "a series of powerful documentaries about the impact of the War on Terror." Think Progress is part of the Center for American Progress, one of the major pro-Obama Soros-funded groups in Washington, D.C.

When a terrorist attack took place on two Canadian soldiers, Snowden collaborator Glenn Greenwald wrote an article titled, "Canada, At War for 13 Years, Shocked That 'A Terrorist' Attacked Its Soldiers [9]." Echoing his 9/11 comments about America, he said about Canada: "It is always stunning when a country that has brought violence and military force to numerous countries acts shocked and bewildered when someone brings a tiny fraction of that violence back to that country."

In other words, Canada inspired this terrorism against

its own people.

Greenwald went on, "If you want to be a country that spends more than a decade proclaiming itself at war and bringing violence to others, then one should expect that violence will sometimes be directed at you as well."

This is how Snowden's accomplice Greenwald sees the world—when the West defends itself against terrorism, the West is guilty of terrorism.

By sheltering Snowden and refusing to turn him over to face espionage charges, Moscow is also implicated in the Islamist war against the West.

One "scoop" from Greenwald was that the NSA had been "targeting" innocent Muslim Americans. One of the individuals allegedly under surveillance was Nihad Awad of the Council on American Islamic Relations (CAIR), a Muslim Brotherhood spin-off.

The Muslim Brotherhood has been banned in Egypt, and three reporters working for its television channel, Al Jazeera, were jailed on terrorism-related charges. Another Muslim American allegedly under NSA surveillance was linked to a terrorist financing case.

As writer Joel Himmelfarb has noted, CAIR was listed as an unindicted co-conspirator in the Holy Land Foundation terrorist financing case, and testimony in the trial showed that its founder, Omar Ahmad, and its current executive director and co-founder, Nihad Awad, both participated in a 1993 meeting of Hamas sympathizers and Holy Land officials in Philadelphia. He noted that additional evidence produced at the trial illustrated the links between CAIR, Hamas and the Muslim Brotherhood.

In another case, Greenwald's public relations firm breathlessly trumpeted the news that "In an exclusive dispatch published this morning, The Intercept reveals top-secret documents from the Edward Snowden archive [that] detail how the NSA has provided financial assistance, weapons, and signals intelligence (SIGNIT) to Israel—enabling attacks on its neighbors, including those on Gaza."

The "neighbors" turned out to be Hamas terrorists.

The Intercept is Greenwald's new media venture, funded by billionaire eBay founder and French-born, Iranian-American Pierre Omidyar.

What the documents show is that the NSA and Israel have been cooperating to identify terrorists. This is precisely what they should be doing.

The headline, "Cash, Weapons and Surveillance: the U.S. is a Key Party to Every Israeli Attack,"[10] appeared over the Greenwald story. This is only a big deal if you're someone like Glenn Greenwald, who thinks it is inappropriate for governments of the Free World to protect their own people.

Greenwald, an American, doesn't live in the United

States; he lives in Brazil with his homosexual lover. He was quoted as saying, "[t]he new Snowden documents illustrate a crucial fact: Israeli aggression would be impossible without the constant, lavish support and protection of the U.S. government, which is anything but a neutral, peace-brokering party in these attacks. And the relationship between the NSA and its partners on the one hand, and the Israeli spying agency on the other, is at the center of that enabling."

Greenwald says it is Israeli "aggression" to defend itself from terrorism.

Although Greenwald insists that innocent Palestinians have been targeted, his own reporting discloses that the NSA and the Israeli signals intelligence unit (ISNU) have shared information with "the Palestinian Authority Security Forces." Clearly, therefore, the target of this intelligence activity is Hamas, the designated terrorist group behind rocket attacks against Israel. The Palestinian Authority had been at odds with Hamas over representing Palestinians.

Greenwald discussed another "top-secret document" that he says deals with a 2009 cooperative effort, code named "YESTERNIGHT," by the NSA, GCHQ (the British Government Communications Headquarters), and ISNU. Greenwald says this "cooperative surveillance-sharing relationship" with Israel coincided with the 2009 "Cast Lead" armed conflict with terrorists in Gaza.

Again, Greenwald seems to be alarmed that the U.S. and Israel would cooperate against terrorism.

Edward Lucas, a journalist who understands and exposes Russian intelligence and espionage operations, wrote a column for the Wall Street Journal under the headline, "A Press Corps Full of Snowdenistas." He described the acolytes of Snowden in the Western press as "utterly paranoid about their own governments, strangely trusting about the aims of the Kremlin." He wrote *Deception. The Untold Story of East-West Espionage Today,* and *The Snowden Operation: Inside the West's Greatest Intelligence Disaster.*

Lacking definitive proof, Lucas does not charge that the Russian intelligence agency, the FSB, was directly behind Snowden from the get-go. Instead, he convincingly argues that Russian intelligence manipulated Snowden through third parties such as WikiLeaks and Glenn Greenwald. This does not mean, he emphasizes, that Snowden's collaborators were "conscious agents" of Moscow. Instead, they operate in a certain "propaganda environment" in which "political movements in the West can serve the Kremlin's purpose without hands-on control."

Lucas doesn't provide all of the necessary detail to understand what this current "political environment" is, although he accuses Snowden's collaborators of having an "anti-American" bent. That is an understatement. We have documented that Greenwald had been a regular participant in communist conferences and spoke to the Council on American-Islamic Relations, a Muslim Brotherhood front. The "Snowdenistas" in the media have failed to report on his pattern of associations with enemies or adversaries of the United States.

These days, many anti-American forces are openly doing what the Soviets and the KGB used to do secretly. Al Jazeera and Moscow-funded RT (Russia Today) television are clearly part of this campaign. Since it is out in the open, some journalists apparently think all of this is legitimate "journalism" and not tainted by any possible association with foreign intelligence services.

In 1960, when NSA analysts Bernon F. Mitchell and William H. Martin defected to the Soviet Union, they held a news conference with Soviet officials in Moscow to spill their secrets. They knew they wouldn't be able to find a journalist willing to publicize their stolen secrets and make them into heroes. Snowden worked mostly through intermediaries like Poitras, Greenwald, and Barton Gellman of The Washington Post. These Pulitzer Prizes for espionage were announced in New York City at the Columbia Journalism Building, in front of a reproduction of the World Building Stained Glass Window that carries the title of "Liberty Lighting the World " But liberty didn't benefit from Snowden; Russia, China, and Islamic terrorists did.

I had asked Sig Gissler, administrator of the prizes: "You said Joseph Pulitzer would approve of these

NSA stories because he wanted the press to be a watchdog. He also said he wanted the press to be a moral force that would promote public virtue. What about the argument that these NSA stories are based on espionage activity by somebody who stole documents who is in the custody of a foreign government committing aggression abroad? Do you think Joseph Pulitzer would approve of that?"

Gissler replied: "I don't know whether he would or not. But the focus of these stories was really on the information that was made available to the public. It really wasn't focused on Mr. Snowden." The "information that was made available to the public" was stolen by Snowden and has enabled Russia to invade Ukraine, and ISIS to rise in the Middle East. The next development, courtesy of Snowden, could be another 9/11 attack on America.

President Eisenhower labeled Mitchell and Martin traitors, and former President Harry Truman said they should be shot. The Obama administration did not label Snowden as a traitor. Congress has a unique opportunity to define the term "treason" and those who engage in it by holding public hearings into the damage being done by Snowden and his collaborators. A new House Internal Security Committee could hold these hearings.

The Snowden Legal Support Apparatus

The Freedom of the Press Foundation, which includes Snowden's media mouthpiece and handler Glenn Greenwald on its board, acknowledges that the organization "is made possible by the fiscal sponsorship of the Foundation for National Progress." This group is best known as the publisher of Mother Jones magazine, and is backed by several prominent liberal foundations, including the Open Society Institute of billionaire George Soros, according to its 2010/2011 annual report.

Mother Jones journalists accepted an award named in honor of I.F. Stone, who postured as an "independent" journalist but was exposed as a Soviet agent of influence.[11] Greenwald had previously received the award.[12]

Snowden is their new hero. "At the heart of Edward Snowden's decision to expose the NSA's massive phone and Internet spying programs was a fundamental belief in the people's right-to-know," said actor John Cusack on the website of the Freedom of the Press Foundation. Cusack is also a member of its board.

The Freedom of the Press Foundation, which openly funnels money to WikiLeaks and Julian Assange, says it is a 501(c)(3) nonprofit organization, and that the Foundation for National Progress "provides users a way to give tax-deductible donations."

"We are pleased to receive anonymous donations in the mail," it says.

One purpose of the arrangement is to make sure that WikiLeaks has a secure funding source, as "U.S. officials unofficially pressured payment processors to cut WikiLeaks off from funding in late 2010, despite the fact that the organization has never been charged with a crime," the group claimed.

In fact, U.S. officials regarded WikiLeaks as hostile to the United States because it publicly released classified counter-terrorism information from Army analyst Bradley Manning, now known as Chelsea, who went to prison. Assange, who called Snowden a "hero," went to work for Moscow-funded television.

The radical left, including members of Barack Obama's "progressive" base, rallied around Snowden, even as Obama himself gave lip service to what the NSA is doing.

One of the prominent directors of the Foundation for National Progress that is backing Snowden is Susan S. Pritzker, a member of one of the richest families in the United States, the Pritzker family, which is very close to Obama. The Pritzker family owns the Hyatt Hotel chain.

Another member of the family, Penny Pritzker, is a Chicago billionaire who was nominated by President Obama and became Secretary of the Commerce

Department. Her nomination was held up because of questions from Senator Charles Grassley (R-IA) about income generated from an offshore account.

The Freedom of the Press Foundation board includes not only Glenn Greenwald of the British Guardian, but Laura Poitras. It was Poitras and Greenwald who had arranged the secret interview with Snowden in Hong Kong and authored the Guardian's story about him. Poitras also shared the lead byline with former Post journalist Barton Gellman on the front-page NSA story in The Washington Post.

The Freedom of the Press Foundation promotes Snowden as a whistleblower, rather than a traitor, as do "journalism and transparency organizations" such as WikiLeaks, the Center for Public Integrity, and the National Security Archive, the latter two of which are funded by George Soros.

Another member of the Freedom of the Press Foundation's board is Josh Stearns, the Journalism and Public Media Campaign Director at Free Press, a Soros-funded group started by Marxist Professor Robert. W. McChesney.

Free Press launched a petition campaign demanding that Congress investigate the National Security Agency's terrorist surveillance activities, labeled "spying programs."

"Stand up for privacy and push Congress to dig up the truth about the NSA's surveillance schemes," the left-wing group says. "Millions of Americans have woken to the threat the NSA's programs pose to our civil liberties."

A "Stop Spying on Us" website was launched, featuring "A Network of Groups Across the Political Spectrum, Organizing against Surveillance Abuse, Government Repression, and Political Witch Hunts; and Working to Expand Civil Liberties, Free Speech, and the Right to Dissent for All."

The National Lawyers Guild, once identified as a Communist front, is playing a key role in the effort.

Another coalition, "Stop Watching Us," included conservative groups such as Freedom Works and the Competitive Enterprise Institute, in addition to MoveOn.org, Electronic Frontier Foundation, and Greenwald's Freedom of the Press Foundation.

Contained in several stories about one of Snowden's meetings in Moscow was the name of his key German contact, a member of the German Green Party, Hans Christian Ströbele, who is also a member of the German Parliament. Buried in some of these accounts is the fact that Ströbele is a prominent German lawyer who represented the communist terrorist group, the Baader-Meinhof Gang—also known as the Red Army Faction (RAF).

Incredibly, Ströbele is now a member of a German parliamentary committee that oversees German intelligence agencies. He has sent letters to the U.S.

House and Senate intelligence committees proposing a "dialogue between both of our monitoring committees and their members and to discuss future changes in the intelligence policy." It's extremely doubtful the U.S. Congress will favorably respond to his initiatives. But the Congressional Progressive Caucus may find his offer appealing.

In Germany, this far-left pro-communist and pro-terrorist lawmaker has significant influence. He is leading a campaign to have the German government protect Edward Snowden by giving him asylum in Germany.

His biography refers to the RAF terrorist killers as "political prisoners." [13]

The book, *Tolerating Terrorism in the West: An International Survey*, notes that Ströbele had been sentenced to 10 months imprisonment in 1982 for setting up a communications network between the prisoners of the RAF and activists outside the jails.[14] He claims this was because of his "mission as a defender" of the RAF prisoners from 1970-1975. Ströbele says the sentence was changed to probation.

In Moscow, Ströbele handed Snowden the "Honorary Diploma of the Whistleblower Award 2013," in honor of his theft and release of classified documents on NSA surveillance programs.

Ströbele's immediate purpose was to get the former NSA contractor—who has been granted temporary political asylum in Russia—to leave Moscow and testify before a German parliamentary committee hearing on the details of NSA surveillance in Europe.

Ströbele's representation of the RAF, whose members were trained at Palestine Liberation Organization (PLO) camps, demonstrates that members of the international communist left in Germany, as well as the U.S., have not disappeared, but in some cases have assumed positions of power and influence. The RAF was the German equivalent of the Weather Underground in the U.S.

The RAF kidnapped and murdered German corporation executives, bankers, and police; bombed U.S. military bases; and attacked U.S. military personnel in Europe in the 1970s and 80s. One of their victims was U.S. Army Specialist Edward Pimental, who was abducted and executed with a bullet to the back of his head. One of his terrorist killers was released in 2007. "The prisoners should have the chance for a new life," Stroebele said, referring to the terrorists being released from prison.

The famous KGB archivist, Col. Vasili Mitrokhin, revealed in the book, *The Sword and the Shield*, that the Soviet KGB, mostly through the East German intelligence service, was behind this campaign of violence and terrorism by the Baader Meinhof Gang/RAF. The purpose was to undermine the U.S. and the NATO Alliance—of which Germany is a member—in Europe.[15]

Egged on by Snowden and his communist backers, Brazil and Germany introduced a U.N. General Assembly "anti-spying" resolution urging all countries to recognize "internationally guaranteed rights to privacy to the Internet and other electronic communications," as The Washington Post described it.

A German magazine, *Die Welt*, reported that high-ranking German security sources say the meeting in Moscow between Snowden, Ströbele, and the others was organized and monitored by the Russian FSB, the successor to the KGB. "This plays into the hands of the Russians," a German intelligence officer said about the campaign to have Snowden come to Germany and testify. [16]

The Soviet Union always sought to divide the U.S. from Germany and its other allies in NATO and Europe. The Putin regime in Russia is using Snowden to try to accomplish the same thing.

The story gets even more interesting when you consider that one of the more detailed accounts of Ströbele's visit with Snowden in Moscow appeared in the People's World, the newspaper of the Communist Party USA, and that the author, Victor Grossman, is an American communist who defected to East Germany and wrote a book about it.

Ströbele is described in the article as "always (or almost always) the Green deputy opposing wars in Iraq, Kosovo, Afghanistan, Patriot missiles for Israel, who fought hardest against anti-foreigner discrimination (even supporting the right of immigrant-rooted police officers to wear turbans or head cloths) and a Turkish version of Germany's national anthem."

Another member of the German Green Party is Joseph Martin "Joschka" Fischer, the German foreign minister and vice chancellor from 1998-2005, under former Chancellor Gerhard Schroder. Fischer was a supporter of the Baader-Meinhoff Gang and attended a 1969 meeting of the Palestine Liberation Organization at which the PLO dedicated itself to the destruction of Israel.

One participant in the Moscow meeting with Snowden was John Goetz, identified as an American journalist living in Germany and associated with a website called "Secret Wars," which purports to know how the U.S. war on terror is conducted from covert bases in Germany. Goetz is now representing Süddeutsche-Zeitung, a major German newspaper.

According to Victor Grossman, Goetz "did a series on Germany's secret assistance to the U.S. war in Iraq" and helped expose the "extraordinary renditions" of anti-American terrorists to secret locations that required German government cooperation.

Other participants in the meeting were Georg Mascolo, a former editor in charge of crime, terrorism, and intelligence issues at Der Spiegel, the German news magazine, and Sarah Harrison of

WikiLeaks.

WikiLeaks posted silent videos of the Moscow meeting.

Snowden's Moscow-based lawyer is another interesting character in this process. Anatoly Kucherena, described as "linked" to FSB and "Kremlin-connected," says his client has accepted a job with a Russian website and that he is studying Russian.

In an article from 2002, written in honor of Russian President Vladimir Putin's fiftieth birthday, Kucherena praised Putin, a former Soviet KGB officer, as a "reformer," reports Deutsche Welle, a German broadcasting company that has covered some of the controversial aspects of the Snowden affair. Kucherena emerged as "one of Vladimir Putin's most prominent supporters and campaigned for him" in 2012, the news organization reported.[17]

Jesselyn Radack, the National Security and Human Rights Director of the Government Accountability Project (GAP), has emerged as a "legal adviser" to Snowden. She traveled to Moscow to meet with Snowden and was on the CBS "Face the Nation" program to rebut charges that Snowden has engaged in espionage against the U.S.

She is a Washington, D.C. lawyer who posed for Playboy while at Yale Law School and was honored at the notorious Playboy Mansion for her work defending another disgruntled NSA employee.

GAP is an offshoot of the Institute for Policy Studies (IPS), an organization that facilitated the activities of CIA defector Philip Agee, who participated in Soviet KGB operations against the U.S.

In one of her many controversial statements, Radack said at an anti-NSA press conference that it would "totally be proper" for the Russian intelligence service, the FSB, to be "guarding" Snowden in Moscow. [18]The FSB is a successor to the Soviet KGB and maintains the Russian surveillance state. Radack also told the press conference that it would be "inappropriate" for the NSA to be conducting surveillance of Snowden.

Some of the press conference participants, who were veterans of the NSA, were questioned about why Snowden went to Moscow. Radack, sitting in the audience, was called upon to explain why he did not go to a country such as Norway, Sweden or Germany.

Radack has explained Snowden's travel to Russia through Chinese Hong Kong as just a quirk in scheduling out of Hawaii, where he was based, with no real political significance. "Hong Kong was an easy flight" from Hawaii, she has said. She blames the U.S. for having "stranded him" in Moscow by revoking his passport when he arrived in Russia.

She went further at the anti-NSA press conference, insisting that Snowden "has been granted political asylum based on a valid fear of persecution by the United States for his "political opinion" and, "therefore, it is perfectly appropriate that—if the FSB were guarding him—that would totally be proper because he has been granted asylum by Russia under the Universal Declaration of Human Rights, to which the U.S. is a signatory."

So the FSB, which is notorious for staging terrorism blamed on Islamists and killing Russian President Putin's political enemies, is somehow guaranteeing Snowden's human rights in Moscow. (Information about the FSB's role in the 1999 Moscow apartment bombings blamed on Islamic terrorists is in our 2014 book, *Back from the Dead: The Return of the Evil Empire.*)

Radack claimed in a *Wall Street Journal* column defending Snowden against espionage charges that "The Espionage Act is for spies like Aldrich Ames and Robert Hanssen, who sold secrets to enemies for profit" and not for Snowden. Ames and Hanssen were paid to spy for Moscow.[19]

But top State Department official Alger Hiss, convicted of perjury for denying he was a Soviet spy, betrayed America for communist ideology, not profit.

Another absurd claim Radack made is that there is "no tangible proof of any damage" from Snowden's disclosures.

Radack goes beyond defending Snowden to affirming

the basis for what Russia has done in this case. Putin "is behaving rationally in protecting Edward Snowden," Radack told me in an interview in October. "Russia's not controlling him in any way." [20]

Now, however, the story has changed, and the FSB apparently is "guarding" him for a perfectly legitimate reason.

Anti-NSA "Scoops" Which Fell Flat

Some of Greenwald's most sensational claims about unwarranted NSA surveillance fell flat, such as in the cases of Dilma Rousseff of Brazil and Angela Merkel of Germany. Greenwald reproduces in his book, *No Place to Hide*, a document showing U.S. interest in the "communication methods" of and "key advisers" to Rousseff, as if this is a hideous use of U.S. surveillance power.

Any serious journalist without an automatic anti-American bias would have to concede that there are legitimate national security grounds to monitor Rousseff and Merkel.

For Greenwald, however, it is "egregious" that Rousseff, a former communist terrorist, would be under surveillance. Rousseff, the daughter of a Bulgarian communist, was described in her police file as a terrorist and bank robber. She now runs Brazil with the support of the Brazilian Communist Party.

"The Baader-Meinhof are long gone in Germany," noted one writer. "In Brazil, they're running the country." [21] The Baader-Meinhof gang was a communist terrorist group.

Another source, WikiLeaks, considered to be more friendly to Greenwald, noted that a U.S. Embassy memo had described Rousseff as the "Joan of Arc of Subversion" when she became chief of staff to her predecessor, Luiz Inácio Lula de Silva of the

Worker's Party of Brazil. WikiLeaks says the memo was "signed by U.S. ambassador John Danilovich," and that it says this about Rousseff's past: "Joining various underground groups, she organized three bank robberies and then co-founded the guerrilla group 'Armed Revolutionary Vanguard of Palmares.'"

Not surprisingly, another WikiLeaks cable said Rousseff "quashed" anti-terrorism legislation, despite evidence of Islamists active in the country. Indeed, one cable referred to "the presence and activities of individuals with links to Terrorism—particularly several suspected Sunni extremists and some individuals linked to Hizballah—in Sao Paulo and other areas of southern Brazil."

Is the NSA not supposed to be monitoring members of terrorist groups who take over huge countries in Latin America? Not in Greenwald's world, where enemies of America and their priorities take precedence.

Yet, Rousseff's speech to the United Nations in 2013 included the audacious claim, "We reject, fight and do not harbor terrorist groups."

Seizing on Snowden's leaks, Rousseff said, "Recent revelations concerning the activities of a global network of electronic espionage have caused indignation and repudiation in public opinion around the world." She said, "Tampering in such a manner in the lives and affairs of other countries is a breach of

International Law and, as such, it is an affront to the principles that should otherwise govern the relations among countries, especially among friendly nations."

Brazil has since emerged as a member of the BRICS alliance of nations.

An article about the BRICS—Brazil, Russia, India, China and South Africa—says they "are becoming less willing to accept US world supremacy." Indeed, this is the name of the game. The objective of Greenwald is to undermine America's influence and standing in the world.

Greenwald also treats German chancellor Angela Merkel's reported outrage over the NSA "eavesdropping on her personal cell phone" as an indictment of the NSA's practices.

Merkel "angrily likened U.S. surveillance to the Stasi, the notorious security service of East Germany, where she grew up," he says. Grew up? She spent 35 years of her life under the surveillance of the Stasi. What's more, the sensational book, *The First Life of Angela M,* [22] suggests Merkel concealed her work as an ideologue for the East German regime's communist youth group. It would not be surprising if U.S. intelligence analysts suspected Merkel was a communist "mole" whose meteoric rise in the ranks of the German elite was something to be extremely concerned about.

Not surprisingly, Greenwald has been promoting his

own book, the subject of the forthcoming movie from the 007 producers. "Now for the first time," his website proclaims, "Greenwald fits all the pieces together, recounting his high-intensity eleven-day trip to Hong Kong, examining the broader implications of the surveillance detailed in his reporting for The Guardian, and revealing fresh information on the NSA's unprecedented abuse of power with never-before-seen documents entrusted to him by Snowden himself."

A better attempt at putting the pieces together was found in Edward Jay Epstein's Wall Street Journal article, "Was Snowden's Heist a Foreign Espionage Operation?" [23] This is the aspect of the Snowden affair that most of the media shy away from. Putin's fingerprints are all over Snowden. But what does Putin want in return for giving him up?

Another Obama Prisoner Swap?

The NSA defector, Victor Norris Hamilton, who defected to the Soviet Union in 1963, was found in a psychiatric prison [24] near Moscow in 1992. Perhaps he realized, too late, that he had made a drastic mistake. It is too late for Snowden, unless the Obama administration makes a deal to get him back.

Incredibly, Snowden could be returned, in exchange for the Russian arms dealer Viktor Bout, who is serving a 25-year sentence in U.S. federal prison. He was convicted, among other things, of conspiring to sell weapons to the communist terrorist Revolutionary Armed Forces of Colombia (FARC) to be used to kill Americans in Colombia. The idea of a Bout-Snowden trade first surfaced in 2013.

Attorney General Eric Holder wrote to the Russians promising that Snowden wouldn't be given the death penalty if he returned home. Obama's new Attorney General, Loretta Lynch, should be questioned about whether a swap is currently being negotiated and if she would approve it. Since Putin may be done with Snowden, such a deal makes sense from his perspective. Then the Obama administration could go through the motions of pretending to have Snowden punished for espionage.

The evil genius behind Snowden's defection, with the help of Greenwald and Poitras, was to frame his revelations in terms of alleging that he was a "whistleblower" who was informing the American people that they were being spied upon. Some prominent conservatives and libertarians fell for the ruse, thinking Obama was using the NSA like the IRS, and that the Fourth Amendment was in jeopardy. They erupted in anger and joined various left-right coalitions to demand that the "spying" stop. On Capitol Hill, their champion was Republican Senator Rand Paul, who joined with the ACLU to announce a lawsuit against the NSA. He treated Snowden as the "whistleblower" he claimed to be and actually filed a bill, The Fourth Amendment Restoration Act, based on Snowden's disclosures.

Obama called him a mere "hacker," which sounds bad but not treasonous.

However, Snowden was described as "this generation's Alger Hiss" by former Republican Senator Jon Kyl (AZ). Kyl, who retired from the Senate after the 2012 election, said, "Heroes and whistleblowers don't admittedly steal thousands of classified documents about some of NSA's most sensitive collection activities, give copies of them to the media, flee to that bastion of personal and political freedom, the People's Republic of China, and, in an irony to end all ironies, seek political asylum in Russia." President Reagan's U.N. Ambassador, John Bolton, calls Snowden a traitor.

Lt. Gen. Ion Mihai Pacepa, the highest-ranking Soviet bloc intelligence official ever to defect to the West, said he believed that Snowden "is an agent of the Russian foreign intelligence service."

He said, "Americans say that if you really want to know someone, you should walk a mile in his moccasins. I walked in disinformation shoes over many miles and for many years, and I have good reason to believe that Moscow's 'surprise' about the 'unexpected' arrival in Moscow of NSA leaker Edward Snowden is the product of a disinformation operation. Few outsiders knew that during the Cold War there were more people in the Soviet bloc working for KGB disinformation than for the Soviet army and defense industry put together. Most of this immense disinformation machinery survived, and it will certainly do its best to persuade the rest of the world that Snowden is a small private salesman who acted on his own. The recent revelation that Snowden spent several days hidden in the Russian consulate in Hong Kong will certainly not help the Kremlin to keep its hand in this defection clean for long."

Logan Beirne, author of *Blood of Tyrants: George Washington & the Forging of the Presidency*, noted that "Just as Snowden sought out a position with inside access to the National Security Agency, [Benedict] Arnold lobbied for command of West Point." Beirne added, "Our founding fathers faced men like Edward Snowden. They sentenced them to death."

To the credit of David Gregory, when he was the host of NBC's "Meet the Press," had asked Glenn Greenwald on Sunday's show why HE shouldn't be arrested. He said, "To the extent that you have aided and abetted Snowden, even in his current movements, why shouldn't you, Mr. Greenwald, be charged with a crime?"

Greenwald responded in part by saying, "I think it's pretty extraordinary that anybody who would call themself a journalist would publicly muse about whether or not other journalists should be charged with felonies. The assumption in your question, David, is completely without evidence, the idea that I've aided and abetted him in any way." But the evidence is available for anyone to see. Greenwald was Snowden's handler.

But some of Snowden's disclosures, coming during President Obama's meeting with the Chinese president, and then on the eve of a meeting with Russian President Vladimir Putin, told us everything we needed to know about his motives. He wanted to embarrass the United States and help America's adversaries.

"Without any doubt his case represents a moral victory of Russia and China over America," former Soviet KGB officer Konstantin Preobrazhensky told me. He meant that China and Russia had used Snowden to make the case that the United States was engaged in the same kinds of surveillance practices it charges Russian and China with using. The claim that the NSA was "spying" on Americans was an essential part of this disinformation and propaganda ploy.

The Infiltration of Congress

Not only should the Congress support the NSA, FBI, CIA, and other intelligence agencies, as the security clearance problems are being fixed, but the House and Senate can reconstitute the internal security committees or subcommittees in both chambers that were dismantled by liberals. These committees could examine how a libertarian ideologue like Snowden, a financial contributor to Ron Paul's 2012 campaign for president, got security clearances in the first place.

Congress could also give consideration to a new loyalty program to make sure our high-level federal officials and those in the intelligence community understand what it means to pledge allegiance to the United States of America.

Instead, however, Socialist Senator Bernie Sanders made headlines with his letter to the NSA demanding to know if the spy agency has been monitoring Congress. Not one article dared to ask whether Sanders and other "progressive" members of Congress should be under surveillance because of their contacts with foreign intelligence agencies.

"Is NSA spying on Congress?" asked[25] Sanders. He joined with Republican Senator Rand Paul to demand restrictions on various NSA programs. The Vermont Senator claims to be "independent," but is considered a member of the Senate Democratic Caucus. He was elected to the U.S. Senate in 2006 after serving 16 years in the House of Representatives, and before that as mayor of Burlington, Vermont.

Stories about the Sanders letter to the NSA on possible surveillance of Congress appeared in Politico, The Huffington Post, The Hill, Buzz Feed, Talking Points Memo, CNN and Fox News.

In a sense, the story was a bunch of hype. Like other Americans, certain data about members of Congress is being collected by the NSA, but not searched unless there is evidence of foreign and terrorist connections. Sanders wanted the public to think this is sinister activity.

But no outlet bothered to go beyond Sanders' publicity stunt to determine whether a case can be made that members of Congress, including Sanders himself, should be under investigation or surveillance. The fact is that no elected federal official in the U.S, including the president and members of Congress like Sanders, goes through a security background check.

The FBI is under the control of the Department of Justice and the President, who control its activities, while Congress is notorious about failing to investigate itself.

If any member of Congress should be under surveillance, it should be Sanders. During the 1980s he collaborated with Soviet and East German "peace committees" to stop President Reagan's deployment of nuclear missiles in Europe, in order to counter a massive Soviet strategic nuclear advantage. Sanders had openly joined the Soviets' "nuclear freeze" campaign to undercut Reagan's military build-up.

The name of Bernie Sanders, then identified as former mayor of Burlington, Vermont, even shows up on a list of speakers at a 1989 U.S. Peace Council event to "end the Cold War" and "fund human needs." Other speakers at the U.S. Peace Council event included Rep. John Conyers, a Democrat from Michigan; Gunther Dreifahl of the East German "Peace Council;" Jesse Jackson aide Jack O'Dell; and PLO official Zehdi Terzi.

Congressional hearings in 1982 demonstrated that the U.S. Peace Council was affiliated with the Soviet-controlled World Peace Council and run by the Communist Party USA. It was part of what the FBI called the Soviet "active measures" apparatus, designed to discredit the U.S. and support communist objectives.

The hearings on Soviet active measures featured testimony from Edward J. O'Malley, Assistant Director for Intelligence of the FBI. He said, "The Communist Party, United States of America, also has a number of front or affiliated organizations working to implement Soviet active measures. Foremost among them is the U.S. Peace Council, an affiliate of the World Peace Council. These organizations are often more effective than the CPUSA itself because the American people they are dealing with may not be aware that they are in fact fronts of the CP [Communist Party]."

He testified that the KGB, the Soviet intelligence service, had "clandestinely transferred funds to the CPUSA" on behalf of the Soviet Communist Party, adding, "Several Soviet officials affiliated with the KGB at the Soviet Embassy in Washington, D.C., and the Soviet Mission to the United Nations are in regular contact with CPUSA members and officials of CPUSA front groups. They monitor CPUSA activities and transmit guidance to the CPUSA officials…In 1979…the CPUSA assigned two of its longtime members to establish a U.S. chapter of the World Peace Council…The key leadership positions in the U.S. Peace Council were given to CPUSA members."

Analyst Trevor Loudon reported that, as mayor of Burlington, Sanders hung the Soviet flag in his mayoral office, in honor of the city's Soviet sister city Yaroslavl. (They are still "sister cities" to this day.) Sanders celebrated the victory of the Soviet-backed communist Sandinistas in Nicaragua and made Burlington a "sister city" with the city of Puerto Cabezas in Nicaragua.

In addition to evidence of Sanders' relationship with communist and Soviet front organizations, an FBI memorandum from 1970 examined "contacts between representatives of the Soviet Union and members of staff personnel of the United States Congress." The memo carries the notation "Internal Security— Russia" and lists several senators, including Ted Kennedy of Massachusetts, as being among the Soviet contacts. In fact, dozens of senators and representatives, and hundreds of congressional staff were said to have been contacted by communist officials.

However, 13 senators and representatives—all but three of them Democrats—were listed by name as being preferred by Soviet officials, and targeted. Another senator listed as being among the preferred Soviet contacts was George McGovern of South Dakota, the Democratic presidential candidate in 1972. Another was Walter Mondale of Minnesota, President Jimmy Carter's vice president, who ran against President Reagan in 1984.

The document said that "...the majority of Soviet personnel maintaining contacts on Capitol Hill are either known to us or suspected to be connected with the Soviet Intelligence Services."

The document was obtained by anti-communist researcher Max Friedman after he got it declassified from the John Dean White House files at the National Archives in College Park, Maryland. It is now in the Nixon Presidential Library and Museum in California.

In sending off a letter to the NSA inquiring about its alleged "spying" on Congress, Sanders was apparently counting on the media not to tell people about his own personal history of collaborating with enemies of the United States. The media played along with his stunt.

It is significant that he introduced legislation to put "strict limits" on what he called the "sweeping powers used by the National Security Agency and Federal Bureau of Investigation to secretly track telephone calls by millions of innocent Americans who are not suspected of any wrongdoing."

It is noteworthy that he lists the NSA and the FBI as using these powers. The NSA turns over evidence of foreign connections to the FBI for the necessary follow-up. But one can be sure, as long as a Democratic president occupies the White House, that Sanders and his fellow "progressive" Democrats in Congress will escape the scrutiny of the FBI.

We know, however, that one of the NSA's greatest successes was known as Venona, the code name given to the intercepted and deciphered KGB and GRU (Russian military intelligence) messages between Moscow and the Soviet espionage network in the United States. The project led to the apprehension of such spies as State Department official Alger Hiss.

We need a similar effort today. Some conservatives have belatedly discovered that Obama has Marxist views and a background of being mentored by the pro-Soviet Communist Party operative, Frank Marshall Davis. It is time for all of this to be put on the public record by a new House Internal Security Committee. Re-establishment of this committee will demonstrate that the new Congress means business and that it won't resort to politics as usual and compromise.

All of this requires that the new Congress takes its responsibilities seriously, not only on fiscal issues, but on matters involving the national security and moral integrity of the United States. The liberals will raise a hue and cry, and some conservatives may balk, but it is mandatory and necessary to begin addressing what an old congressional committee used to call "un-American activities" at the highest levels of the U.S. Government.

America's Survival, Inc. has for years been urging the new Congress to reestablish House and Senate internal security committees or subcommittees. The George Soros-funded Center for American Progress acted frightened and alarmed in 2010 when Rep. Steve King (R-IA) expressed agreement with my suggestion at that time that re-establishment of such a committee would be a good idea. "I think that is a good process and I would support it," he said.

The oath of office for members of Congress requires that they support and defend the Constitution of the United States "against all enemies, foreign and domestic."

Donald I. Sweany, Jr., a research analyst for the House Committee on Un-American Activities and its successor, the House Committee on Internal Security, sees the need for such a committee. He has issued this statement:

"The re-creation of the House Committee on Internal Security will provide the Congress of the United States, Executive Branch agencies and the public with essential and actionable information concerning the dangerous and sovereignty-threatening subversive activities currently plaguing America. This subversion emulates from a host of old and new entities of Marxist/Communist revolutionary organizations and allied militant and radical groups, some of which have foreign connections. A new mandated House Committee on Internal Security is of great importance because it would once again recommend to Congress remedial legislative action to crack down on any un-American forces whose goals are to weaken and destroy the freedoms which America enjoys under the Constitution. In addition, this legislative process will provide public exposure of such subversives."

President Ronald Reagan talked openly about the growing Marxist influence in Congress as he battled with congressional liberals to stop the Soviet advance in Latin America.

In fact, as President, he told journalist Arnaud de Borchgrave in a 1987 interview that "I've been a student of the communist movement for a long time, having been a victim of it some years ago in Hollywood." He said that he regarded some two dozen Marxists in Congress as "a problem we have to face."

The problem is far worse today. Analyst Trevor Loudon now counts the number of Marxists in Congress at more than 60, a fact that would seem to make it more imperative to re-establish a committee or subcommittee on internal security. All it would take is more courageous members like Rep. Steve King, backed by the House Leadership. Such a committee would be able to seriously analyze an area that remains off-limits to the House Homeland Security Committee, the House Intelligence Committee, and the Select Committee on Benghazi—subversive infiltration of the highest levels of the U.S. government, including the White House and Congress.

However, leave it to Glenn Greenwald's website the Intercept to publish the article, "The Ghost of Ronald Reagan Authorizes Most NSA Spying," on what they called "a 33-year-old executive order issued unilaterally by President Ronald Reagan." Yes, Greenwald is correct in this case. The fact is that Reagan used an executive order to facilitate and expand the NSA's abilities to assist in the war against Soviet communism.

Reagan fought the Russian communists and used the NSA against them. Greenwald finds this objectionable.

Conservative and Libertarian Dupes

It was expected that the far-left would rally to Snowden's side. It has been shocking to see that radio host Michael Savage called Snowden a "patriot." In addition, Glenn Beck said his disclosures were an "act of heroism," and Joseph Farah said he was a whistleblower who should be given immunity from prosecution by Congress. Craig Shirley, a conservative political consultant in Washington and author of several Ronald Reagan biographies, insisted that, "Support for Snowden is actually consistent with the tradition of American conservatism."

Stealing documents and aiding the enemy is consistent with American conservatism?

Martin Edwin "Mick" Andersen, in his special chapter, dissects the "whistleblower" label as applied to Snowden.

The Snowden case looks increasingly like the NSA equivalent of Philip Agee, who defected from the CIA and became a Soviet and Cuban agent. Agee died in Havana after writing several books with the help of Cuban intelligence. America's Survival, Inc. released Agee's FBI file.

Agee used to travel back and forth to the United States from Cuba. But Jimmy Carter's Justice Department declined to arrest and prosecute him.

Going back further, remember that Communist

Duncan Lee had infiltrated the OSS, the predecessor to the CIA, for the Soviets, and he was never prosecuted or convicted. He was exposed definitively as a Soviet agent by the Venona intercepts of Soviet messages by the NSA.

Venona was one of the great successes of the NSA that the media don't want to talk about. Rather than dismantle the NSA, perhaps we need to beef it up, to develop another Venona project, this time directed at agents of influence for radical Islam and international communism in our own government.

Yet, Andrew Napolitano, a Fox News personality, had proclaimed Snowden an "American hero" and said he "understands that the government listening to half the country is not what was bargained for when statutes were enacted in the days and weeks after 9/11."

In fact, the NSA is not "listening to half the country" but collecting telephone numbers and can only monitor the communications of an American linked to a foreign terrorist when it has probable cause and a court order. Napolitano, a Ron Paul supporter, has been a regular on the Alex Jones radio show, a forum for people who believe the Boston bombings and the 9/11 terrorist attacks were U.S. Government plots.

Incredibly, Fox News' Shepard Smith responded to this diatribe by insisting that the government can "watch everything we do" and even knows "when I'm using my microwave oven."

When Fox News reports this kind of nonsense, which feeds paranoia, you know that accurate and objective coverage of the NSA controversy is a virtual lost cause. That's one reason why my group, America's Survival, Inc., with the assistance of Jerry Kenney of Kenney Broadcasting, began a television program on the Roku streaming device. We provide an alternative source of news and information that is now seen in the U.S. and more than 50 other countries.

One of the worst offenders on Fox News was Eric Bolling, who said the channel was eager to provide a "platform" for further criminal disclosures from Snowden. His remarks came during a Bolling interview of Greenwald. Bolling, a co-host of "The Five," even suggested that Snowden, under indictment for espionage and theft of government property, be brought back to the U.S. to help fix the Obamacare website. This comment was apparently made in jest.

Bolling seemed unaware that Greenwald had made speaking appearances to such groups as the International Socialist Organization and the Council on American-Islamic Relations. The ISO is an openly Marxist-Leninist organization where people chant such things as "Palestine will be free," and "Wars of occupation will never bring liberation." As noted, CAIR is a front group of the Muslim Brotherhood.

"Always great having you on," Bolling said. He said he was "waiting, ready, willing and able to hear what you're ready to break." Greenwald responded. "So generous of you Eric—I really appreciate that."

The warm exchange with a dedicated enemy of the United States was not something that conservatives had come to expect from the Fox News Channel.

Bolling didn't seem interested in exploring the issue of the disclosures making it easier to kill Americans. Instead, he became a cheerleader for Greenwald.

The pattern of hostility to the United States was not something that seemed to bother Bolling, who pleaded for Greenwald to come back on the Fox News Channel to release more of Snowden's information about the NSA's secret surveillance programs.

Greenwald had already paid a visit to the "Fox & Friends" morning program for an interview with Bolling and was urged on that occasion to use the appearance to release more classified information about the NSA. Bolling asked Greenwald if David Gregory of NBC News had "apologized" for suggesting that Greenwald could be prosecuted for his role in helping Snowden make his criminal disclosures. Gregory's question was entirely legitimate. Section 798 of the Espionage Act absolutely prohibits the publication of classified information in the area of communications intelligence. That would include programs of the NSA.

Appearing on "The Five," Bolling said it was "absolutely insane" to suggest that Greenwald be prosecuted. He added, "We need more Glenn Greenwalds. We don't need fewer of them."

On the other hand, Catherine Herridge, chief intelligence correspondent for Fox News Channel, reported on the damage that was done. In a December 2, 2013, report, she said, "A review of the NSA leaks by Fox News shows the majority of the leaks since June now deal with sources, methods and surveillance activities overseas, rather than the privacy rights of American citizens."

In other words, Snowden stole NSA documents and leaked them for the express purpose of weakening America's defenses against terrorism. To put it another way, Snowden was never the "whistleblower" he claimed to be, but has been serving the interests of America's enemies and adversaries.

However, the libertarian Cato Institute took Snowden's side. It published a three-page interview with Greenwald in its July/August 2014 Cato Policy Report. Cato, which opposes a strong U.S. foreign policy, called Greenwald's NSA disclosures "explosive," which is true in the sense that the communications intelligence agencies of countries like the U.S. and Israel have been hobbled by the publicity given to the stolen documents he received and publicized.

Robert A. Levy, chairman of the Cato Institute's

board of directors, wrote that if a deal is worked out, Snowden could return to the U.S. and "be held accountable for other actions, not yet disclosed, that amount to espionage—traditionally defined as transmitting national defense information with intent or reason to believe that it will be used to the injury of the United States or the advantage of a foreign nation."

In view of these comments, not knowing the full extent of the damage he has done, why would Cato give Snowden a platform? His video appearance at a Cato Surveillance Conference had to have been arranged with the help of the Russian security agents who guard Snowden and regulate access to him. Why would Cato participate in such an arrangement?

David and Charles Koch were two "shareholders" in the Cato Institute, and were involved in a lawsuit that resulted in John Allison (the former CEO of BB&T) replacing Ed Crane, who retired as Cato's CEO. According to a press release, "For Charles Koch and David Koch, the agreement helps ensure that Cato will be a principled organization that is effective in advancing a free society."

What this means in terms of Cato's embrace of Snowden should be a matter addressed to the Koch Brothers. Snowden is a captive of Vladimir Putin's Russia, which is definitely not a free society but is a place where Koch Industries does business. (Koch Industries also does business in Communist China.) Do the Kochs approve of Cato's embrace of

Snowden? David Koch, who served as the Executive Vice President of Koch Industries, Inc., continues to serve on Cato's board. Cato's 2013 annual report lists the Charles Koch Foundation as a financial backer.

The Koch-funded Students for Liberty not only gave Snowden its highest honor, its 2014 national conference featured Oliver Stone, now making a film about Snowden. Another Koch-funded youth group, Young Americans for Liberty, featured Snowden's collaborator, Glenn Greenwald, at its 2014 conference.

Analyst Trevor Loudon notes, "When Edward Snowden first made his revelations, it wasn't the left who first rushed to his support—it was the right, including Glenn Beck and Michael Savage. It was completely understandable. In the wake of Obama's IRS and Associated Press scandals, Snowden's revelations were seized on by many on the right as one more example of President Obama's tyrannical bent. Hundreds of bloggers, commentators and grass-roots activists sprang immediately to Snowden's defense, even after it became clear that Snowden was hopping from one enemy-controlled territory to another."

Loudon's book, *The Enemies Within: Communists, Socialists and Progressives in the U.S. Congress* [26] analyzes the career of far-left Democratic Rep. John Conyers (MI), who teamed up with Republican Tea Party Congressman Justin Amash (MI) to sponsor a bill to gut the NSA's terrorist surveillance powers.

The bill almost passed the House.

Loudon says that Rep. Amash, chairman of the House Liberty Caucus, is a patriot whose conservative credentials are beyond question. However, "he should ask himself why an out and out socialist like Conyers would want to limit the powers of the NSA," Loudon says. "Conyers has a more than 40-year history of collaborating with the Communist Party, and almost as long with the Democratic Socialists of America."

This association raises "red flags," he says. Loudon points to how the Communist Party (CPUSA), which was funded by Moscow and engaged in espionage against the U.S. Government, created a front group, the National Committee to Abolish the House Un-American Activities Committee. The House Committee was a target because it had held numerous hearings exposing the activities of the CPUSA and its front groups.

Loudon's research shows that Frank Wilkinson, who was jailed in 1961 for defying the House Committee on Un-American Activities, was "a vocal foe of the FBI's supposedly tyrannical and out-of-control Director J. Edgar Hoover." Wilkinson was in fact a 40-year veteran of the Communist Party USA, an affiliation common to most of his organization's leading supporters. And it turned out that Wilkinson's FBI dossier was more than 130,000 pages long.

Loudon comments: "J. Edgar Hoover's memory has been invoked several times in the current scandal as an example of someone who used government-gathered intelligence to harass and blackmail his personal enemies. As an effective opponent of communist subversion, J. Edgar Hoover suffered a decades' long campaign of slander and denigration from the left. The fact that Hoover had 130,000 pages of information on a pro-Soviet communist activist, who led a long and successful campaign against one of the country's most important anti-subversive organizations, proves that information gathering does not necessarily lead to inappropriate use of that information."

Another figure involved in the anti-FBI campaign was Frank Donner, the former director of the ACLU's Project on Political Surveillance. Donner's FBI file, turned over to America's Survival, Inc., is over 1,500 pages long.

Donner worked with the Center for National Security Studies (CNSS), which is now active against the NSA, to undermine the intelligence-gathering capabilities of the U.S. Government. Donner, like Wilkinson, had a lot to hide, since he was a member of the CPUSA who traveled to Russia and had contacts with Russian espionage agents. He wrote several books attacking U.S. intelligence agencies, including the NSA. He especially hated the House Committee on Un-American Activities, which grilled him on his CPUSA activities. He took the Fifth. But Donner had the last laugh, as the committee and its successor, the House Committee on Internal Security, were abolished in the 1970s.

The same forces are now working against the NSA.

It is noteworthy that in 2012, the George Soros-funded Open Society Institute (OSI) held one of its panel discussions, "National Security Secrecy and Surveillance: Defending the Public's Right to Know," to organize opposition to the NSA. The name of one panelist, Tim Shorrock, rang some bells for me. I had covered his work with CounterSpy, an anti-CIA publication, back in 1983. CounterSpy had exposed Richard Welch as a CIA agent before his murder by terrorists in Greece. Shorrock told me, "Every once in a while, you're going to release a name of somebody who may be the target for somebody. That's something that happens when you do investigations."

At the time, Shorrock told me that he favored the abolition of the CIA, adding, "I don't think the KGB is a threat." He also said, "I support a lot of what the Cuban government does."

In 2009, when we focused critical attention on Glenn Greenwald getting an award named in honor of leftist journalist and identified Soviet agent I.F. Stone, Shorrock came to Greenwald's defense, recalled my interview of him, and denounced me as "a longtime McCarthyite and deranged right-winger, who has been seeing reds under every bed since he was probably an infant."

Turning his attention to the Snowden case, Trevor Loudon notes that reports indicate that in March

2013, when he sought a job with NSA contractor Booz Allen Hamilton at an NSA facility in Hawaii, Snowden presumably signed the required classified-information agreements and would have been well aware of the law and potential penalties for breaching laws regarding the information he would have access to.

Before taking the job in Hawaii, Loudon notes, Snowden had already been in contact with Greenwald and filmmaker Laura Poitras, who serve together on the Board of the Freedom of the Press Foundation, a funder of WikiLeaks.

This is a critical point, reflecting the fact that Snowden could not have engaged in espionage without the help of others, including left-wing networks based in the U.S.

Loudon, who broke the story of former White House official Van Jones' Marxist background, says many left-wing groups backing Edward Snowden have one thing in common—they hate and distrust America. "Many of them have ties to Marxist or anti-American groups," he says. "Some are linked to international communist fronts. Several are tied to hostile foreign regimes. Their agenda in most cases is to weaken America's defenses. Attacking and weakening the NSA would be cheered on by America's enemies all over the globe."

"The United States has always had its enemies in Congress and the media," says Loudon. "What is of most concern is that millions of American patriots, motivated by genuine constitutional concerns, have been turned into attack dogs against one of their few remaining effective means of national defense. America's enemies must be laughing uproariously over this. Political influence on NSA, if any, should indeed be questioned. The constitutionality of its methodology should be debated. But Americans need to turn their guns on those who would gut the NSA, not those would defend it."

In the Service of Vladimir Putin's Gulag

(These remarks were delivered at the "Espionage is Not Journalism" conference sponsored by America's Survival, Inc. on November 17, 2014, in the Zenger Room of the National Press Club in Washington, D.C.)

By Martin Edwin Andersen

It is a pleasure being here with you today. Even though our political views differ significantly, I would like to point out that—as I got to know him in the aftermath of 9/11—Cliff Kincaid has worked hard to promote the rights of real whistleblowers, modern Paul Reveres, in government and out.

I will limit my comments to the question of the whos and whys of real whistleblowing and why Edward Snowden does not make the grade. I should point out that in my own case it was the FBI that came to my aid; for me, the Bureau is like extended family and had it not been for an agent who went on to teach ethics in Quantico, things could have turned out quite different.

It is important to remember in this world's oldest democracy, one that has the American eagle as its national symbol, that you can be left-wing, right-wing or middle of the bird, but lawful protest is a constitutional right.

And as John F. Kennedy once said:

Let every public servant know, whether his post is high or low, that a man's rank and reputation ... will be determined by the size of the job he does, and not by the size of his staff, his office or his budget.

Let it be clear that this Administration recognizes the value of dissent and daring-- that we greet healthy controversy as the hallmark of healthy change.

Unfortunately, one of the most damning criticisms that can be made in discussions among too-often ahistorical Americans is that someone is a "conspiracy theorist"—the challenge referring to someone who presses hard on the paranoia pedal without regard for facts.

The case of national security leaker Snowden puts that putdown on its head ...

It is the "coincidence theorists" who need to come clean about why they have chosen to promote someone now enveloped in the protective embraces of the olympic Russian police-state champion Vladimir Putin.

For many of those used to fighting the good fight from the trenches of good government and public accountability, the strange case of former National Security Agency contractor Snowden causes particular dread.

As the cases of Ukraine, Chechnya and Georgia show, former KGB officer Putin is a master at deception and propaganda; witness his very public embrace of Snowden, who stole classified documents far in excess of those he supposedly took to make his argument against the NSA, and then fled U.S. legal reach.

Even a fierce critic of U.S. foreign policy like actor Sean Penn, who himself defends whistleblower rights, was obliged to note that Snowden was not "legitimate," his acts "based on the narcissism of the so-called 'whistleblower'."

Thus, like a bad dream with no end, a leaker arguably more akin to Edward Everett Hale's "The Man Without a Country" is being promoted around the globe by many who should know better as a brave and selfless "whistleblower."

At stake: the very concept of whistleblowing and whatever chance there is to achieve bipartisan Congressional support for protecting real government truth tellers (modern Paul Reveres), today and in the future.

With Snowden and Company trying to centrally cast him as a 21st Century "hero," the foot soldiers of left, right and center find themselves facing hard choices that will likely mean more pain and hardship for myriad already-overburdened true believers in a government of the people and for the people.

Ironically, aligned in favor of a soft landing for Snowden—someone who clearly decided to commit felonies before he got his last government contractor assignment—are some of the media giants with a record of being most in favor of lawful government openness and accountability; in other words, the very values we hold in common.

Arm in arm and in lock step with The New York Times, the Guardian, the Pulitzer Prize committee and a host of other media are, unfortunately, some important defenders of often-praised but rarely practiced protection for those in government committed to speak truth to power—whistleblowers.

Yet the arguments used in defense of Snowden dangerously parallel those that too many corrupt or narcissistic government bureaucrats—protective of their personal interests and policy preferences rather than those of the voting public—like to trot out in order to stave off real accountability.

The New York Times editorial judgment itself revealed a key dilemma when it said that, "Considering the value of his leaks and the N.S.A. abuses he has exposed, Mr. Snowden should be offered clemency or a plea bargain."

And what happens if the next Snowden acts to promote ideas or values the Times somehow finds unpalatable or repugnant?

Applied more generally, the message seems to be that individuals in a bureaucracy should, from here on, be permitted to engage in criminality if they themselves disagreed with state policy, especially those meaures that are highly unpopular or controversial.

The slippery slope emerges when—following a pardon of Snowden—hundreds of thousands of government workers of many different opinions, values and experiences left, right and center, begin to believe that any government policy about which they have significant disagreement can justifiably be thwarted by felony conduct.

Snowden appears to have no problem portraying himself as judge, jury and bureaucratic executioner—all in a single person.

"I am not trying to bring down the NSA, I am working to improve the NSA," he claimed, as supposed "good government" groups promoted his receiving a Nobel Peace Prize. "I am still working for the NSA right now. They are the only ones who don't realize it."

In fact, embracing Snowden is the good-government-activist equivalent of tainted Kool Aid, or making Stalin an ally—for those who to do so, watch your backs very carefully once the leaker claims to have "won."

Create a system of the promotion of individual lawlessness based on personal ideology while working in the large and complicated bureaucracy and you may very well see both our government and the way of life it is supposed to defend suffer accelerated dry rot.

Some in the good government sphere defending Snowden have rushed to red-hot judgment on how, for example (in the words of a real but kool-aid entranced whistleblower): "Everyone with a security clearance who has access to sensitive information is part of the conspiracy, even if they haven't personally observed wrongdoing, because they have been captured by the secrecy regime."

Basic fact checking on Snowden's activities shows that they have gone far beyond whatever exposure he gave to alleged official illegality (remember, accused bureaucrats also have the right to trial, and an assumption of innocence until proven guilty as well).

Taking advantage of a security clearance whose rules Snowden took an oath to respect and using a set of talents which permitted him to rob some 1.7 million classified documents, this virtual Viet Cong knowingly grabbed bushels of top secret information that—rather than proving violations of citizen rights and federal law—included vital knowledge of legitimate, legal NSA operations meant to protect this country and its people.

Well-regarded national security whistleblower lawyer Mark Zaid has offered insightful analysis about what all of this means, zeroing in on those …

who unequivocally and without hesitation, fully support, without making any factual or legal distinction whatsoever, the illegal conduct of individuals such as ... Snowden.

Some, but not all of course, of those involved on this side argue nothing more than policy rhetoric rather than the actual state of the law.

And rather than use the opportunity to highlight inadequacies in the system AND propose and pursue reform, some merely jump on the bandwagon to make a hero out of unlawful conduct that lawyers, especially whistleblowing lawyers, should be quite wary of promoting.

Clearly our federal system, like many state and local governments, is in vital need of reform to protect truth tellers, particularly national security whistleblowers. Perhaps it is the British whistleblower group, Public Concern at Work, that bests articulates the importance of truth tellers in a free and open society.

Whistleblowing, Public Concern at Work says, "is a valuable activity which can positively influence all of our lives." It then goes on to offer another critical observation: "The whistleblower rarely has a personal interest in the outcome of any investigation into their concern—they are simply trying to alert others."

Snowden's personal interest is all but self-evident. He

did not want to face the music for his actions—even while posing as a champion of civil disobedience in the tradition of Dr. Martin Luther King, Jr., Cesar Chavez and Daniel Ellsberg.

Instead Snowden sought refuge in the olympically-authoritarian Russia, offered other nations even more NSA secrets if they too would help him, and then went on to claim the United States owed him a huge debt of gratitude for wantonly violating its laws.

Only the willingly blind can see this as anything other than theft, not civil disobedience. Even someone like Fareed Zakaria, a self-declared sympathizer of Snowden's, admitted in a *Washington Post* column that none, repeat none, of the leaker's "substantive revelations" resulted in uncovering anything done by the NSA that was "morally scandalous."

And anyway, as far as the rule of law is concerned, you don't end cannibalism by eating alleged cannibals.

As Americans were going to the polls earlier this month, the U.S. Supreme Court was not only making history by hearing the first case involving a federal whistleblower; its ultimate judgment will without doubt be closely followed by Putin's Kremlin, its prized asylum-seeker Snowden, and camp followers such as Glenn Greenwald and Laura Poitras.

In hearing oral arguments involving Robert MacLean's disclosure of post-9/11 cracks in U.S. air passenger security, the high court was asked to consider what was already seemingly decided by a unanimous federal appeals court ruling.

That court found, as did the U.S. Office of Special Counsel (the agency that was so helpful in my own case) in favor of the former air marshal, who was retaliated against by nervous bosses who accused him of making a disclosure "specifically prohibited by law."

Nonetheless the government maintains that MacLean's 2003 unclassified leaks to the media about illegal action at the Transportation Security Administration (TSA) were themselves prohibited—due to imagined catastrophic consequences.

This despite the fact that MacLean, who like myself has been defended by the Government Accountability Project, has garnered impressive bi-partisan support in Congress from conservatives and liberals, Democrats as well as Republicans.

Putin, Snowden and others whose actions continue to threaten U.S. national security are likely rubbing their hands in delight, given the possibilities left wide open by the government's position.

Unlike Snowden, who leaked massive amounts of national security information, then fled to Russia—a police state where, the State Department reports, real whistleblowers and investigative journalists alike are under continuous threat—MacLean stayed here and, despite an arduous legal process that left him nearly broke, went on to win in a court of law.

Those who know the former armed plain-clothes TSA officer who guarded commercial airplanes argue persuasively that MacLean's efforts were meant to help prevent terrorist attacks.

What MacLean did caused the TSA to rollback a planned cut, supposedly for budget reasons, in overnight missions—a cutback due to occur in the wake of air marshals having been just briefed on a "potential plot" to hijack U.S. planes.

(The whole argument of cutting back on national security for budget reasons was questionable on its face. Even as MacLean was being reprised against, myself and Tim Starks, another reporter at Congressional Quarterly, broke the story that the TSA was hosting an employee "celebration"—or party— that cost more than $200,000. It was that story that caused the legendary DHS Inspector General Clark Ervin, a George W. Bush appointee, to start an investigation.)

MacLean's disclosures were factual and they shed light on a TSA action that itself was arguably a violation of federal law—it is supposed to give protective priority to "nonstop, long-distance flights" which are high security risks. That his disclosures "evidenced a substantial and specific danger to public health or safety" there can be no doubt.

In a strictly forthright world, one might think that Putin, Snowden and their crypto-insurgent fellow travelers in the press would be hoping that MacLean would win his case in the highest court of the land.

Snowden has wrapped himself in a "freedom of expression" banner, and nothing in his case against the NSA has motivated greater, if factually flatulent, public debate than that. As the world continues to speculate on the extent of the intelligence bonanza enjoyed by the former KGB maven, what is clear has been Putin's savvy use of the Snowden affaire to ridicule the United States.

Only the willingly blind can see this as anything other than criminal theft, not civil disobedience. As far as the rule of law is concerned, you don't end cannibalism by eating alleged cannibals.

MacLean's service as a real whistleblower placed him and his family at substantial risk as he stayed here and fought to have his rights recognized in a court of law. Hence, the rub.

Prominent Snowden fans embrace—some as if on cue—the much-different MacLean and his cause while the Supreme Court begins to meditate its final resolution. Their solidarity, however, should be suspect.

The raison d'etre for being a whistleblower—telling truth to power in the public interest—already ratified by a federal appeals court in the case of MacLean, obviously was not there in what Snowden did, despite the vociferous arguments of the anti-U.S. crowd. Wonton lawlessness on behalf of one's political ideas, or "world view," does not ethical dissent make.

A high court decision that permanently martyrs a real whistleblower like MacLean offers Putin and Co. the kind of propaganda ammo they most desire but could not buy—the ability to point to a documented case of official illegality without the possibility of legal recourse in the world's oldest democracy.

This as Putin, Snowden and others seek to press their case for their own morally scandalous behavior.

(Note: MacLean won his case before the Supreme Court 7-2, in an opinion by Chief Justice Roberts on January 21, 2015. Justice Sotomayor filed a dissenting opinion, in which Justice Kennedy joined.)

* * * *

The July 30, 1778 Resolution of the Continental Congress states unequivocally…That it is the duty of all persons in the service of the United States, as well as all the other inhabitants thereof, to give the earliest information to Congress or other proper authority of any misconduct, frauds or misdemeanors committed by any officers or persons in the service of these states, which may come to their knowledge.

National security whistleblowers—those working outside the Beltway and without the same access to

Congress, the media, expert legal counsel, and the opportunity for face-to-face meetings with the Office of Special Counsel that I had and Bobby MacLean has—need to have appropriate legal protections in place in order to survive.

While I am personally no more important than I was at the beginning of my own whistleblower process, I think my experience does offer a case study of what real whistleblowing—as opposed to Snowden's leaking—does, in the words of the Continental Congress ...

> to give the earliest information to Congress or other proper authority of any misconduct, frauds or misdemeanors committed by any officers or persons in the service of these states, which may come to their knowledge.

[1] How Edward Snowden Changed Journalism:
http://www.newyorker.com/news/daily-comment/snowden-changed-journalism.

[2] Pulitzer Prizes for Espionage: http://www.aim.org/aim-column/pulitzer-prizes-for-espionage/

[3] openly discussed: http://www.aim.org/aim-column/glenn-greenwald-calls-weakening-of-america-a-very-good-thing/

[4] article:
http://www.washingtontimes.com/news/2014/sep/4/islamic-state-using-edward-snowden-leaks-to-evade-/

[5] joint bipartisan statement: http://intelligence.house.gov/press-release/hpsci-chairman-mike-rogers-and-ranking-member-ca-dutch-ruppersberger-%E2%80%9Csnowden%E2%80%99s-acts

[6] http://www.fbi.gov/philadelphia/about-us/history/famous-cases/famous-cases-robert-lipka-an-american-spy

[7] https://citizenfourfilm.com/

[8] interview:
http://www.youtube.com/watch?feature=player_embedded&v=218hx0dn3so#!

[9] Canada, At War for 13 Years, Shocked That 'A Terrorist' Attacked Its Soldiers:
https://firstlook.org/theintercept/2014/10/22/canada-proclaiming-war-12-years-shocked-someone-attacked-soldiers/

[10] Cash, Weapons and Surveillance: the U.S. is a Key Party to Every Israeli Attack:
https://firstlook.org/theintercept/2014/08/04/cash-weapons-surveillance/

[11] accepted an award: http://www.aim.org/aim-column/soviet-agent-award-for-mother-jones-reporter/

[12] received: http://www.aim.org/aim-column/izzy-award-sends-blogger-into-a-tizzy/

[13] biography: http://www.stroebele-online.de/person/biographie/index.html

[14] Tolerating Terrorism in the West: An International Survey:
http://www.amazon.com/Tolerating-Terrorism-West-International-Survey/dp/0415024412

[15] The Sword and the Shield: http://www.amazon.com/The-Sword-Shield-Mitrokhin-Archive/dp/0465003125

[16] reports:

http://www.welt.de/print/die_welt/politik/article121503461/Hat-der-FSB-Stroebeles-Besuch-organisiert.html

[17] reports: http://www.dw.de/snowdens-lawyer-is-putin-fan/a-17208837

[18] Radack said:
https://www.youtube.com/watch?v=J1u3_IUGbpU&feature=c4-overview&list=UUukW9fbX4m5MpOmQ2M5isVg

[19] column:
http://online.wsj.com/news/articles/SB200014240527023035954045793188840056986684

[20] told me: https://www.youtube.com/watch?v=OL3wHxaYIs4

[21] noted one writer:
http://www.therival.com.au/index.php/brazil-dilma-rousseff/

[22] The First Life of Angela M: http://www.dw.de/merkel-hiding-things-in-her-past-biographer-says/a-16813375

[23] Was Snowden's Heist a Foreign Espionage Operation?:
http://online.wsj.com/news/articles/SB10001424052702304831304579542402390653932

[24] http://www.nytimes.com/1992/06/04/world/american-defector-is-found-in-russian-prison.html

[25] asks: http://www.sanders.senate.gov/newsroom/recent-business/is-nsa-spying-on-congress

[26] The Enemies Within: Communists, Socialists and Progressives in the U.S. Congress:
http://pacificfreedomfoundation.org/